The Post Office

Mary O'Keeffe

GILL EDUCATION

Here we are at the **post office**!

Have you been in the **post office** before?

There are lots of things that you can do in your post office, including sending letters, buying stamps and even topping up your mobile phone!

We can do a lot in here.

Are you ready? Let's go in!

When you go to the **post office**, you have to wait. There are lots here, so you have to wait your turn.

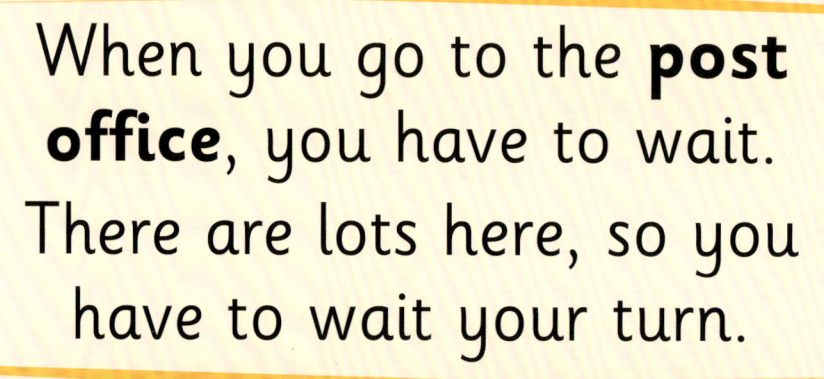

One by one, you will get to the top. When it is your turn, you can go up to the desk.

This is the GPO. It is Ireland's biggest post office and is situated right in the heart of Dublin City, on O'Connell Street.

When you get to the top, she will help you. She can tell you what has to be paid.

She can tell you what your letter will cost to post.

She will let you post your gifts.

She can do a lot for you.

He has a box to post to Nan in the UK.

It did not fit in the post box, so he had to go to the **post office**.

What did it cost to post?

Mam put a tag on the box.
Can you see where
the box has to go?

The box will be put in the van with post from the post box.

It will go here.
The man will
see the tag.

The box
will go to
the next
van now.

The man will put
the box in the van.

The box will go on a boat.
The boat will go to the UK.
Then, the box will go here.

The box is in the sorting office now.

The man will see where the box has to go.
He will put the box on a big belt.
He will load up all of the boxes.

The box will go into the red van. The red van will go to Nan's.

The postal service in the UK is called the Royal Mail.

Uh-oh! The box will not fit!

Looks like Nan will have to go to the **post office** to get it!

When will you go to the post box?

What will you put in the post?

Will you have to go to the **post office**?